HARD
QUESTIONS

I0661190

about
Christianity
made easy

Mark Water

HENDRICKSON
P U B L I S H E R S

Hard Questions About Christianity Made Easy
Hendrickson Publishers, Inc.
P.O. Box 3473,
Peabody, Massachusetts 01961-3473

Copyright © 2000 John Hunt Publishing
Text copyright © 2000 Mark Water

ISBN 1-56563-527-2

Designed and produced
by Tony Cantale Graphics

First printing - June 2000
Reprinted 2002

Manufactured in Hong Kong/China

Unless otherwise noted,
Scripture quotations are taken
from HOLY BIBLE, NEW
INTERNATIONAL VERSION
copyright © 1973, 1978, 1984
by International Bible Society.
All rights reserved.

Photography supplied by
Digital Stock, Digital Vision,
Foxx Photos, Goodshoot,
PhotoAlto, Photodisc and
Tony Cantale

Illustrations by
Tony Cantale Graphics

Contents

Special pull-out chart

"Aren't there some tough questions that Christianity has no satisfactory answer to?"

WHAT'S THE PROBLEM?

"Some problems, like the suffering of the innocent, have vexed the minds of the greatest Christian theologians down the centuries. Isn't this an insuperable barrier to belief in a good God? How can you give any *Made Easy* answers to such block-busting questions?"

ADMIT THE SIZE OF THE PROBLEM

There are some difficulties which do not appear to have any satisfactory answers. In humility, we have to admit this. On the next few pages we will examine some of these tough questions.

MAKE USE OF THE LIGHT YOU HAVE

1. STUDY THE BIBLE

Some of the "Tough Questions" will be fully and satisfactorily answered in the Bible.

"Study to shew thyself approved unto God, a workman that needeth not to be ashamed, rightly dividing the word of truth." *2 Timothy 2:15 KJV*

2. REFLECT ON THE TEACHINGS OF JESUS AND THE PRINCIPLES UNDERLYING HIS TEACHINGS

When people ask: "What is God like?" Christians reply, "Look at Jesus. Look at his life, his healings, his teachings, his death and resurrection." When people ask: "What does Christianity teach?" Christians reply, "Check and see what Jesus the supreme Teacher had to say on this topic?"

3. RELY ON THE HOLY SPIRIT

"The philosophers of old made reason the sole ruler of man and listened only to her, as the arbiter of conduct. But Christians make reason move aside and give complete submission to the Holy Spirit." *John Calvin*

Ask for the Holy Spirit's help as you tackle these "Hard Questions".

4. DISCUSS THESE TOUGH QUESTIONS WITH CHRISTIAN FRIENDS

If you belong to a Christian group discuss some of these questions together.

WHAT'S THE CONCLUSION?

Christians have a duty to answer (to the best of their ability) any genuine questions about their faith.

"But in your hearts set apart Christ as Lord. Always be prepared to give an answer to everyone who asks you to give the reason for the hope that you have. But do this with gentleness and respect."
1 Peter 3:15

A QUOTE TO CHEW OVER

"But when he, the Spirit of truth, comes, he will guide you into all truth." *John 16:13*

"Doesn't all the suffering in the world prove there is no God?"

WHAT'S THE PROBLEM?
"How could a good and loving God allow evil and suffering in his world? Would not an all-powerful God remove all suffering from his world? The conclusion is obvious: the existence of evil and suffering in the world certainly proves that there is not a loving and powerful God."

WHY DOESN'T GOD JUST ZAP ALL EVIL?
If God destroyed all the evil in the world where would that leave us? None of us claim to be perfect, or totally free from evil. So if God removed all evil from the world would any human beings be left?

WHY BLAME GOD FOR EVIL AND SUFFERING?
There's no logic in saying that suffering is God's fault. God is not responsible for creating evil and pain. When God created the world he created a wonderful world. It had no evil or suffering in it. "God saw all that he had made, and it was very good." *Genesis 1:31*

MOST SUFFERING IS SELF-INFLICTED
C.S. Lewis reckoned that over 95% of all suffering in the world can be traced back to the evil actions of human beings. Who is responsible for all the children who have had their legs blown off by stepping on a land mine? Who do we blame for not feeding the starving when there is enough food in the world for everyone? Who is to blame for the spread of AIDS? Why build cities near active volcanoes?

GOD'S ANALYSIS OF HUMAN BEINGS

"The Lord looks down from heaven
    on the sons of men
to see if there are any who understand,
    any who seek God.
All have turned aside,
    they have together become corrupt;
there is no one who does good,
    not even one."
Psalm 14:2-3

GOD HIMSELF KNOWS ALL ABOUT SUFFERING

Not only does God know all about suffering, he suffered himself. God is no stranger to pain. When God, in Jesus, became one of us, he experienced suffering just as we do.

Tertullian, the second century theologian, thinking of Jesus' death on the cross, referred to God as "The crucified God".

When Jesus died in agony on the cross, "God was reconciling the world to himself in Christ."
2 Corinthians 5:19

WHAT'S THE CONCLUSION?

Surely the hope of heaven puts human suffering into a new context?

"I consider that our present sufferings are not worth comparing with the glory that will be revealed in us."
Romans 8:18

A QUOTE TO CHEW OVER

"God whispers to us in our pleasures, speaks in our conscience, but shouts in our pains; it is his megaphone to rouse a deaf world."
C.S. Lewis

"Why discount other religions in favor of Jesus Christ?"

WHAT'S THE PROBLEM?

"Christians say that Christianity is superior to all other religions in the world because of Jesus. That seems rather narrow and intolerant. Anyway, what's so special about Jesus and Christianity?"

JESUS IS UNIQUE

Christians don't say that Jesus was just a little bit better than any other prophet. They say that Jesus was like no other religious leader – that Jesus was totally unique.

Note three of the ways in which Jesus is like no other.

1. JESUS IS UNIQUE BECAUSE OF HIS QUALIFICATIONS

In the second Christian sermon preached, Peter said of Jesus:

- He is the "Holy and Righteous One" *ACTS 3:14*
- He is the "author of life". *ACTS 3:15*
- He is the one whom all the Old Testament prophets spoke about. *ACTS 3:18*
- He is "the Christ". *ACTS 3:20*

2. JESUS IS UNIQUE BECAUSE OF HIS ACHIEVEMENT

The New Testament teaches that Jesus is the world's Savior because he can forgive our sins, and so bring us into fellowship with God. Jesus did this when he died on the cross. "He [Jesus] himself bore our sins in his body on the tree [the cross], so that we might die to sins and live for righteousness." *1 PETER 2:24*

3. JESUS IS UNIQUE BECAUSE OF HIS RESURRECTION

Because of his resurrection it is possible for us to know Jesus Christ today. He did not decay in some grave in Jerusalem. He rose from the dead and is alive today. Muslims cannot claim to know Muhammad. Hindus cannot claim to know Buddha. But ... all Christians are able to say with Paul, "I know whom I have believed." *2 TIMOTHY 1:12*

The focus of the first Christian sermons reached their climax with the resurrection of Jesus.

- The first sermon: "You, with the help of wicked men, put him [Jesus] to death by nailing him to the cross. But God raised him from the dead." *ACTS 2:23-34*
- The second sermon: "You killed the author of life [Jesus], but God raised him from the dead." *ACTS 3:15*
- The third sermon: "It is by the name of Jesus Christ of Nazareth, whom you crucified but whom God raised from the dead, that this man stands before you healed." *ACTS 4:10*

A Buddhist does not say that Buddha is a Savior

The English Buddhist, Maurice Walsh, has pointed out that the Buddhist view of Buddha is quite different from the Christian view of Christ. "Buddha is a Teacher – not a Savior."

A Muslim does not say that Muhammad is a God

"No one in the Islamic world has ever dreamed of, according to Muhammad, divine honors – he would have been the first to reject any such suggestion." STEPHEN NEIL

9

"What about those who have never heard?"

WHAT'S THE PROBLEM?

"Jesus said, 'No one comes to the Father except through me' (*John 14:6*). So the only way to have forgiveness of sin and everlasting life is through Jesus. So are those who have never heard of Jesus now condemned to hell?"

GOD IS EVERYONE'S JUDGE

• **Everyone will have to be judged by God**

"He [God] has set a day when he will judge the world with justice." *Acts 17:31*

• **God is a just judge**

"He will judge the world in righteousness and the peoples in his truth." *Psalm 96:13*

• **God will not make any mistakes**

Human judges are not perfect; sometimes they make mistakes. Innocent people have been given the death penalty.

When God judges us he will never make a mistake. He will never condemn an innocent person. Nobody will be able to accuse God of being unfair. So although we may not know how God will judge a particular person, we do know that he will be fair. And when it comes to those who have never even heard about Jesus, we can be assured that God will be flawlessly and graciously just.

PEOPLE WILL BE JUDGED ACCORDING TO THE LIGHT THEY HAVE BEEN GIVEN

• **We all have to answer to our conscience**

Nobody will ever be condemned because he or she has not heard about Jesus Christ. All people will be judged in the light of their obedience to the moral standards they are aware of.

"All who sin apart from the law will also perish apart from the law, and all who sin under the law will be judged by the law. For it is not those who hear the law who are righteous in God's sight, but it is those who obey the law who will be declared righteous. (Indeed, when Gentiles, who do not have the law, do by nature things required by the law, they are a law for themselves, even though they do not have the law, since they show that the requirements of the law are written on their hearts, their consciences also bearing witness, and their thoughts now accusing, now even defending them.) This will take place on the day when God will judge men's secrets through Jesus Christ, as my gospel declares." *Romans 2:12-16*

• God says nobody will have any excuse to offer on judgment day

"Since what may be known about God is plain to them, because God has made it plain to them. For since the creation of the world God's invisible qualities – his eternal power and divine nature – have been clearly seen, being understood from what has been made, so that men are without excuse." *Romans 1:19, 20*

GOD CARES ABOUT THE SALVATION OF PEOPLE MORE THAN WE DO

• God's fervent wish is that everyone should be saved

"He [the Lord] is patient with you, not wanting anyone to perish, but everyone to come to repentence." *2 Peter 3:9*

WHAT'S THE CONCLUSION?

"Christ sent me to preach the gospel and he will look after the results." *Mary Slessor*

A QUOTE TO CHEW OVER

"I exhort you, press on in your course, and exhort all men that they may be saved." *Polycarp*

• God cares so much about all people that he sent Jesus

"For God so loved the world that he gave his one and only Son, that whoever believes in him shall not perish but have eternal life." *John 3:16*

IT APPEARS THAT SOME PEOPLE HAVE BEEN SAVED WHO KNEW LITTLE ABOUT GOD

• Cornelius, before he heard about Jesus, was commended

Peter said, "I now realize how true it is that God does not show favoritism but accepts men from every nation who fear him and do what is right." *Acts 10:34-35*

• Rahab, the prostitute, appears to have known little about God but was accepted by God because of her faith. *Joshua 2:8-13; Hebrews 11:31*

"Can sincere non-Christians get to heaven?"

WHAT'S THE PROBLEM?
"Won't God accept people who are very religious and totally sincere even if they are not Christians?"

YOU CAN BE SINCERE, BUT SINCERELY WRONG

Some people think that God will accept them because they lead decent, upright lives. But the Christian faith hinges on God's forgiveness of our sins, not on what we may have done for others. Proverbs 14:12 warns, "There is a way that seems right to a man, but in the end it leads to death."

THE TRUTH TEST IS MORE IMPORTANT THAN THE SINCERITY TEST

Other people who openly admit that they are not Christians and who say they worship some other god expect to be accepted by God when they die. The prophet Isaiah taught that the God of the Bible is the *only* God, when he said, "O Lord Almighty … you alone are God over all the kingdoms." *Isaiah 37:16*

Just being a sincere, religious person is not the standard God uses. God judges according to TRUTH.

THERE IS ONLY ONE WAY TO GOD

God has made the way to him quite clear. It is through Jesus Christ. There is no other route.

"Salvation is found in no one else, for there is no other name under heaven given to men by which we must be saved."
Acts 4:12

DO "VERY NICE" PEOPLE NEED SALVATION?

C.S. Lewis wrote,

"A world of nice people, content in their own niceness, looking no further, turned away from God, would be just as desperately in need of salvation as a miserable world – and might even be more difficult to save."

WHAT'S THE CONCLUSION?

A person can be sincere, but he/she also can be sincerely wrong.

A QUOTE TO CHEW OVER

"There is a way that seems right to a man, but in the end it leads to death." *Proverbs 16:25*

"Now that we live in a scientific age, haven't we outgrown Christianity?"

WHAT'S THE PROBLEM?

"Christianity was founded in a pre-scientific age. It was OK for then, but we've come of age now. Do we have need for such outdated ideas in the 21st century?"

SCIENCE VERSUS THE BIBLE

Contrary to popular perception, there is no conflict between science and the Bible. The Bible contains many verifiable facts, such as Nebuchadezzar, Babylonian king, besieging and destroying Jerusalem.

Different aims

However, science and the Bible have different purposes. Science is a body of knowledge which has been carefully acquired by observation, experiment and induction. God's purpose in the Bible is to reveal truths which could never have been discovered using scientific tools. Had it not been for the Bible, we would never have known fully about God's love.

Science – truly amazing, yet restricted

Science has transformed our world in countless wonderful ways. But science does not help us to discover the meaning of life.

The intention of science

"Since the Holy Spirit did not intend to teach us whether heaven moves or stands still, nor whether the earth is located at its center or off to one side, then so much the less was it intended to settle for us any other conclusion of the same kind.

"Now if the Holy Spirit has purposely neglected to teach us propositions of this sort as irrelevant to the highest goal (that is, to our salvation), how can anyone affirm that it is obligatory to take sides on them?

"I would say here something that was heard from an ecclesiastic of the most eminent degree: 'The intention of the Holy Spirit is to teach us how one goes to heaven, not how heaven goes.'" *Galileo*

Evolution

Many Christians believe that the theories of evolution go against the teaching of the Bible. However, scientists who are Christians do not believe that there is any conflict between scientific discoveries and the teaching of the Bible.

God is not a theorem

"God is not a theorem; he is a person. As such, he is only known and encountered in a total relationship which involves and affects not only our mind but the life and character as well. To know God's dossier is nothing; to know him is everything." *R.T. France*

LEADING SCIENTISTS WHO WERE ALSO DEVOUT CHRISTIANS

ARTHUR SCHAWLOW
Professor of Physics at Stanford University who shared the 1981 Physics Nobel Prize for the development of laser spectroscopy
Schawlow has said, "It seems to me that when confronted with the marvels of life and the universe, one must ask why and not just how. The only possible answers are religious. I find a need for God in the universe and in my own life."

JOHN GLENN
Astronaut
From his spacecraft Glenn observed, "Looking at the earth from this vantage point [of the moon], looking at this kind of creation and to not believe in God, to me, is impossible. To see (earth) laid out like that only strengthens my beliefs."

HENRY "FRITZ" SCHAEFER
Graham Perdue Professor of Chemistry and director of the Center for Computational Quantum Chemistry at the University of Georgia
Professor Schaefer, a five-time nominee for the Nobel Prize who has also been cited as the third most quoted chemist in the world, said, "The significance and joy in my science comes in those occasional moments of discovering something new and saying to myself, 'So that's how God did it.' My goal is to understand a little corner of God's plan."

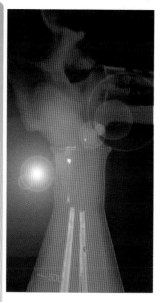

WHAT'S THE CONCLUSION?
Science is not a barrier to belief.

"A legitimate conflict between science and religion cannot exist. Science without religion is lame; religion without science is blind." *Albert Einstein*

A QUOTE TO CHEW OVER
The discoverer of chloroform, Sir James Young, was once asked: What is the greatest discovery you ever made? He replied:

"The greatest discovery I ever made was that I was a great sinner and Jesus Christ a wonderful Savior."

"Does Christianity welcome or reject 'New Age' teaching?"

WHAT'S THE PROBLEM?
"Don't "New Age" ideas combine the best elements of Christianity with Eastern religion? There's so much in it that sounds great: holistic health, care for the environment, world peace and self-improvement programs. So why don't all Christians become New Agers?"

IS THE NEW AGE MOVEMENT VERY WIDESPREAD?
One survey maintains that 25% of Americans are involved in some way in the New Age movement.

WHAT IS THE NEW AGE MOVEMENT?
1. The New Age Movement is a broad, social, spiritual, and intellectual movement.
2. It is based on the religious philosophy of the Far East.
3. Some of its practices involve dabbling in and/or being immersed in the occult.

WHAT KINDS OF THINGS DO NEW AGE FOLLOWERS INDULGE IN?
- Tarot cards
- Fortune-telling
- Mediums
- Channeling
- Astrology
- Clairvoyance
- Spiritism
- Pyramids
- Horoscopes
- Spirit guides
- Consulting the dead
- Crystals

DOES IT SEEK TO WIN CONVERTS?
"The battle for humankind's future must be waged and won in the school classroom by teachers who correctly perceive their role as the proselytizers of a new faith. The classroom must and will become an arena of conflict between the old and the new – the rotting corpse of Christianity and the new faith of Humanism."
New Ager, John Dynphy

PANTHEISM

The people of the Far East have long been pantheistic in their understanding of reality. They believe that God is in all things and (in a sense) all things are divine – a part of God.

The New Age philosophy, based on pantheism, has been summarized by John Stott as saying: "All is God" "All is one" "All is well."

A CHRISTIAN REPLY

In contrast to this New Age teaching, theism teaches that "in him [God] we live and move and have our being" (*Acts 17:28*). It is through the death of Christ that healing and peace are given, and the disease of the world healed.

WHAT'S THE CONCLUSION?

New Age salvation is self-salvation. New Age forgiveness is self-forgiveness. In complete contrast to this, Jesus said: "I am the way and the truth and the life. No one comes to the Father except through me." *John 14:6*

A QUOTE TO CHEW OVER

"See to it that no one takes you captive through hollow and deceptive philosophy." *Colossians 2:8*

"Haven't we outgrown belief in the devil?"

WHAT'S THE PROBLEM?
"Does anybody still believes in the existence of an impish figure with a forked tale? Isn't it a childish evasion of responsibility on the part of Christians."

SATAN AND THE DEVIL
"Satan" is the Hebrew word for adversary. The word "Satan" is mentioned 36 times in the New Testament. "Devil" comes from the Greek word *diabolos* meaning accuser or slanderer. The word "devil" appears 33 times in the New Testament.

SATAN'S OTHER NAMES ALSO REVEAL HIS CHARACTER

Name	Example of name being used	Bible reference
1. Accuser	"The accuser of our brothers"	Revelation 12:10
2a. Great dragon 2b. Ancient serpent	"The great dragon was hurled down – that ancient serpent called the devil."	Revelation 12:9
3. Beelzebub	"Beelzebub, the prince of the demons"	Matthew 12:24
4. Belial	"What harmony is there between Christ and Belial?"	2 Corinthians 6:15
5. The evil one	The evil one snatches away God's word.	Matthew 13:19
6. Prince of this world	"The prince of this world will be driven out."	John 12:31
7. Ruler of the kingdom of the air	"When you followed the ways of the world and of the ruler of the kingdom of the air."	Ephesians 2:2

JESUS AND SATAN

Jesus	Versus	Satan
1 Jesus Christ is God		Satan is a created being.
2. "The Son of God appeared		to destroy the devil's work." 1 John 3:8
3. Jesus was tempted in the desert		by the devil. Matthew 4:1-11
4. Jesus showed his superiority over the devil		when he successfully resisted him.
5. Through Jesus' death and resurrection		Satan's power over us is shattered

"And having disarmed the powers and authorities, [Christ] made a public spectacle of them, triumphing over them by the cross." *Colossians 2:15*

"So that by his death he might destroy him who holds the power of death - that is, the devil – and free those who all their lives were held in slavery by their fear of death." *Hebrews 2:14-15*

WHAT'S THE CONCLUSION?

"The existence of the devil is so clearly taught in the Bible that to doubt it is to doubt the Bible itself." *Archibald G. Brown*

A QUOTE TO CHEW OVER

"There is nothing that Satan more desires than that we should believe that he does not exist." *Bishop Wordsworth*

"Isn't demon-possession really mental illness?"

WHAT'S THE PROBLEM?

"We know so much more today about medicine than was known 2,000 years ago. Aren't the instances of so-called demon possession in the New Testament what we would call mental illness today?"

ENTER DR LUKE

It's most helpful that we should have a qualified medical doctor as one of the writers of the Gospels. He would have known the difference between mental illness and demon-possession and noted the difference.

DEMON POSSESSION AND OTHER ILLNESSES DISTINGUISHED

Luke is not confused

He distinguishes between demon-possession and other illnesses.

"At that very time Jesus cured many who had diseases, sicknesses and evil spirits, and gave sight to many who were blind." *Luke 7:21*

Jesus is not confused

He spoke directly to demons within a person.

"Be quiet. Come out of him." *Mark 1:28*

DEMON POSSESSION

In the New Testament demon possession means that a person is dominated by the spirit of a demon and tormented by him.

The demons are expelled

1. The demoniac in the synagogue at Capernaum.	MARK 1:21-28
2. The dumb demonic	MATTHEW 9:32-34
3. The daughter of the Canaanite woman	MATTHEW 15:21-28; MARK 7:24-30
4. The Gadarene demoniacs	MATTHEW 8:28-34; LUKE 8:26-39
5. The blind and mute demoniac	MATTHEW 12:22; LUKE 11:14
6. The epileptic child	MATTHEW 17:14-21

WHAT'S THE CONCLUSION?

"There are two equal and opposite errors into which our race can fall about devils. One is to disbelieve in their existence. The other is to believe, and to feel an excessive and unhealthy interest in them. They themselves are equally pleased by both errors and hail a materialist or a magician with the same delight." *C.S. Lewis*

A QUOTE TO CHEW OVER

"Like a good chess player Satan is always trying to maneuver you into a position where you can save your castle only by losing your bishop." *C.S. Lewis*

"If Satan does exist, so what?"

WHAT'S THE PROBLEM?

"Most people don't believe in Satan. But what difference would it make to anyone if he did exist?"

THE ACTIVITIES OF SATAN

"Know your enemy" is the advice of many successful military commanders. Satan's actions reveal what he does as the enemy of God and of God's followers.

1. He stops unbelievers from believing

"The god of this age has blinded the minds of unbelievers, so that they cannot see the light of the gospel of the glory of Christ."
2 Corinthians 4:4

2. He is the Christian's enemy

"Your enemy the devil prowls around like a roaring lion looking for someone to devour. Resist him, standing firm in the faith.
1 Peter 5:8-9

3. He is a murderer

"He was a murderer from the beginning." *John 8:44*

4. He has no truth in him

"He [does] not hold ... to the truth, for there is not truth in him." *John 8:44*

5. He is a liar

"When he lies, he speaks his native language, for he is a liar and the father of lies." *John 8:44*

6. He leads the whole world astray

"The devil, or Satan ... leads the whole world astray."
Revelation 12:9

7. He is at work in the hearts of non-Christians

"The spirit who is now at work in those who are disobedient."
Ephesians 2:2

HOW ARE CHRISTIANS TO WIN AGAINST THE DEVIL?

1. Resist him
"Resist the devil, and he will flee from you." *James 4:7*

2. Come close to God
"Come near to God and he will come near to you." *James 4:7*

3. Be always clothed in God's armor
Christians are engaged in a fierce spiritual battle.

a. Note what the fight is against.
"Put on the full armor of God so that you can take your stand against the devil's schemes. For our struggle is not against flesh and blood, but against the rulers, against the authorities, against the powers of this dark world and against the spiritual forces of evil in the heavenly realms."

b. Note the armor that is to be put on.
"Therefore put on the full armor of God, so that when the day of evil comes, you may be able to stand your ground, and after you have done everything, to stand.
1. Stand firm then, with the belt of truth buckled round your waist,
2. with the breastplate of righteousness in place,
3. and with your feet fitted with the readiness that comes from the gospel of peace.
4. In addition to all this, take up the shield of faith, with which you can extinguish all the flaming arrows of the evil one.
5. Take the helmet of salvation and
6. The sword of the Spirit, which is the word of God."

Ephesians 6:10-17

PRAYER
Prayer is the Christian's resource against Satan and demons.

"And pray in the Spirit on all occasions with all kinds of prayers and requests." *Ephesians 6:18*

WHAT'S THE CONCLUSION?

"I am certain that one of the main causes of the ill state of the church today is the fact that the devil is being forgotten. We have become so psychological in our attitude and thinking. We are ignorant of this great objective fact – the being, the existence of the devil, the adversary, the accuser." *Martyn Lloyd-Jones*

A QUOTE TO CHEW OVER

"The best way to drive out the devil, if he will not yield to texts of scripture, is to jeer and flout him, for he cannot bear scorn." *Martin Luther*

"Was Jesus any more than a good moral teacher?"

WHAT'S THE PROBLEM?
"Jesus was just a great moral teacher. Why should we, today, be concerned about anything he did or said?"

1. THE INFLUENCE OF JESUS' LIFE
Even non-Christians agree that:
• Jesus lived a wonderful life.
• He has influenced thinking, music and art more than anyone else over the past 2,000 years.
• He is responsible for our values and the West's system of justice and education.
• Today we date everything from the start of the Christian era.

2. YES, JESUS WAS A GOOD MORAL TEACHER – HE TAUGHT ABOUT PAYING TAXES:

> "Give to Caesar what is Caesar's, and to God what is God's." *Matthew 22:21.*

He gave revolutionary teaching about a proper attitude towards one's enemies:

> "You have heard that it was said, 'Love your neighbor and hate your enemy.'But I tell you: Love your enemies and pray for those who persecute you." *Matthew 5:43-44.*

He taught us to help all people in need, even those we don't know: The parable of the Good Samaritan ends with the words, "Go and do likewise." *Luke 10:37*

3. BUT, JESUS WAS MORE THAN A TEACHER OF MORALS

Jesus claimed that:

• **He would give his life as a ransom for many.**

"The Son of Man did not come to be served, but to serve, and to give his life as a ransom for many." *Mark 10:45*

• **He would rise from the dead.**

"Don't tell anyone what you have seen, until the Son of Man has been raised from the dead." *Matthew 17:9*

• **He would judge people on judgment day.**

"Many will say to me on that day, 'Lord, Lord, did we not prophesy in your name, and in your name drive out demons and perform many miracles?' Then I will tell them plainly, 'I never knew you. Away from me, you evildoers!'" *Matthew 7:22-23*

WHAT'S THE CONCLUSION?

A mere good teacher of morals would hardly claim to die for others, come back to life and then be our judge after this life.

A QUOTE TO CHEW OVER

"Take hold of Jesus as a man and you will discover that he is God." *Martin Luther*

"Was Jesus deluded?"

WHAT'S THE PROBLEM?
"Christians claim that Christianity stands or falls by Christ. So, what if Jesus was deluded? Wouldn't that blow Christianity sky high?"

1. WAS JESUS JUST PLAYING MAKE BELIEVE?
That creates more problems that it solves.
- **Problem 1**
Jesus was totally opposed to any type of hypocrisy. Could he have allowed his whole life to be built on a lie?
- **Problem 2**
Put yourself in the shoes of a phony, bogus preacher. Would you be prepared to be killed by one of the most agonizing deaths ever invented, if you knew you were only pretending?

2. WAS JESUS JUST MISTAKEN?
Was he psychologically unbalanced?
That also creates problems.
Problem 1
Could anyone who was mentally off or emotionally mixed-up give such incredible teachings?
Problem 2
Could a person suffering from delusions of grandeur show such selfless love to so many close friends?

DOES A MADMAN?
- Does a madman go round healing mad people?
- Does a mental case go round performing miracles?
- Does a silly fool give logical and awe-inspiring sermons?

WEIGH THE EVIDENCE
Jesus expelled demons from "Legion" (a madman) who:
- tore apart the chains that bound him
- broke in pieces the shackles that held him
- screamed wherever he went
- roamed through burial caves
- cut himself with stones
Mark 5:1-20 37

SOME SERIOUS STUDY

• Miracles performed by Jesus are recorded in Matthew, Mark, Luke and John.

• Have you ever read any religious writing that compares with Jesus' Sermon on the Mount (*Matthew 5–8*)? It begins with the beautiful beatitudes. "Blessed are the poor in spirit, for theirs is the kingdom of heaven." *Matthew 5:3*

A QUOTE TO CHEW OVER

"If Jesus is not the one who makes God real to us by sharing our human nature, he is either an untrustworthy liar or a deluded imbecile." *Michael Green*

"Was Jesus more than a carpenter?"

WHAT'S THE PROBLEM?

"There are so many conflicting opinions and views about who Jesus really was and what he did. Can we be sure he was such a great guy? After all, even his family did not believe in him."

JESUS AS CRAFTSMAN

"Jesus himself did not come from the proletariat of day-laborers and landless tenants, but from the middle class of Galilee, the skilled workers. Like his [foster] father, he was an artisan, a *tekton*, a Greek word which means mason, carpenter, cartwright and joiner all rolled into one."
Professor Martin Hengel

ONE SOLITARY LIFE

"He was born in an obscure village, the child of a peasant woman. He worked in a carpentry shop until he was 30, and then for three years he was an itinerant preacher. When the tide of popular opinion turned against him, his friends ran away. He was turned over to his enemies. He was tried and convicted. He was nailed upon a cross between two thieves. When he was dead, he was laid in a borrowed grave.

"He never wrote a book. He never held an office. He never owned a home. He never went to college. He never traveled more than 200 miles from the place where he was born. He never did one of the things that usually accompanies greatness.

"Yet all the armies that ever marched, and all the governments that ever sat, and all the kings that ever reigned, have not affected life upon this earth as powerfully as has that One Solitary Life."
Author unknown

DISCOVER WHO THE REAL JESUS IS FOR YOURSELF

The best and quickest way to gain an accurate picture of the life of Jesus is to read the Gospels.

• Matthew's Gospel presents Jesus as the Christ, Israel's messianic King.

• Mark's Gospel presents Jesus as the Servant who came to give his life a ransom for many.

• Luke's Gospel presents Jesus as the perfect Son of Man whose mission was to seek and save the lost.

• John's Gospel presents Jesus as the eternal Son of God who offered eternal life to all who put their trust in him.

A QUOTE TO CHEW OVER

"The life of Christ is more wonderful than the greatest miracle."
Lord Alfred Tennyson

"How could Jesus be both human and divine?"

WHAT'S THE PROBLEM?
- "If Jesus were God, he could hardly be a normal human being.
- "If Jesus were a man, he could hardly have been God. You can't have it both ways. Either he was God or man – how could he be both at the same time?"

AN IMPOSSIBLE PROBLEM?
This seems to be an impossible problem for anyone to solve. The only resort is to see what the Bible teaches about this.

1. The Bible teaches that Jesus is God

The Father said so:	"This is my Son, whom I love; with him I am well pleased." Matthew 3:17
Peter acknowledged this:	"You are the Christ, the Son of the living God." Matthew 16:16
Paul taught it:	"For in Christ all the fullness of the Deity lives in bodily form." Colossians 2:9
The writer to the Hebrews affirmed it:	"But in these last days he has spoken to us by his Son, whom he appointed heir of all things, and through whom he made the universe. The Son is the radiance of God's glory and the exact representation of his being, sustaining all things by his powerful word." *Hebrews 1:2-3*

2. The Bible teaches that Jesus is man

Jesus experienced, first hand, ordinary human feelings.

Jesus tasted sorrow:	"He [Jesus] took Peter and the two sons of Zebedee along with him, and he began to be sorrowful and troubled." *Matthew 26:37*
Jesus grew physically:	"And the child grew and became strong." *Luke 2:40*
Jesus suffered hunger:	"He [Jesus] ate nothing during those days, and at the end of them he was hungry." *Luke 4:2*
Jesus needed sleep:	"So they [the disciples and Jesus] got into a boat and set out. As they sailed, he [Jesus] fell asleep." *Luke 8:22*
Jesus got tired:"	Jacob's well was there, and Jesus, tired as he was from the journey, sat down by the well." *John 4:6*
Jesus knew what it was to be tempted:	"For forty days he was tempted by the devil … [the devil] left him until an opportune time." *Luke 4:1,13*

WHAT'S THE CONCLUSION?

"He ate, drank, slept, walked, was weary, sorrowful, rejoicing, he wept and laughed; he knew hunger and thirst and sweat; he talked, he toiled, he prayed … so that there was no difference between him and other men, save only this, that he was God and had no sin." *Martin Luther*

A QUOTE TO CHEW OVER

"The Jesus of the gospels, precisely as a human being, believed himself called to do things, and to be things, which only make sense if it was God himself who was doing them and being them." *Dean Tom Wright*

"Did Jesus really claim to be any more than just a first century rabbi?" (1)

WHAT'S THE PROBLEM?

"There seems to be great confusion about just who Jesus was. Theologians in the world's most prestigious universities disagree among themselves. How are we meant to come to a conclusion about Jesus?"

LOOK AT THE CLAIMS OF JESUS

You may not agree with all or anything that Jesus said, but that should not stop you from viewing the evidence dispassionately.

The best sources to find out about Jesus are the four portraits of Jesus written up by Matthew, Mark, Luke and John.

THE CLAIMS OF JESUS IN MATTHEW'S GOSPEL

• Jesus claimed to forgive sins.
"The Son of Man has authority on earth to forgive sins." *Matthew 9:6*

• Jesus claimed to be able to tell God the Father who belongs to him.
"Whoever acknowledges me before men, I will also acknowledge him before my Father in heaven." *Matthew 10:32*

• Jesus claimed to be able to reveal God the Father to people.
"All things have been committed to me by my Father. No one knows the Son except the Father, and no one knows the Father except the Son and those to whom the Son chooses to reveal him." *Matthew 11:27*

• Jesus claimed to be able to give people rest if they came to him.
"Come to me, all you who are weary and burdened, and I will give you rest." *Matthew 11:25-26*

• Jesus offered an alternative "yoke" to the "yoke of the law" given by the Pharisees.
"Take my yoke upon you and learn of me." *Matthew 11:29*

THE CLAIMS OF JESUS IN MARK'S GOSPEL

• **Jesus claimed to be master of the Sabbath.**
"The Son of Man is Lord even of the Sabbath." *Mark 2:28*

• **Jesus claimed that he came to give his life for others and so rescue them.**
"For even the Son of Man did not come to be served, but to serve, and to give his life as a ransom for many." *Mark 10:45*

QUOTES TO CHEW OVER

Unbelievers

LORD BYRON, PROFLIGATE POET
"If ever man was God,
or God was man,
Jesus Christ was both."

SPINOZA, APOSTATE JEW
"Jesus Christ was the Temple; in him God has most fully revealed himself."

RT. HON. W. LECKY OF DUBLIN, HISTORIAN
"Christ has exerted so deep an influence that it may be truly said that the simple record of three short years of active life has done more to regenerate and soften humankind than all the disquisitions of philosophy, and all the exhortations of morality."

J.J. ROUSSEAU, ATHEIST
"If the life and death of Socrates were those of a sage, the life and death of Jesus were those of a God."

Believers

JAMES MARTINEAU
"Jesus Christ must be called the Regenerator of the human race."

W.E. GLADSTONE
"All that I live for is based on the divinity of Christ."

THOMAS B. MACAULAY
"Deity embodied in human form."

ANONYMOUS
"It would take a Jesus to forge a Jesus."

"Did Jesus really claim to be any more than just a first century rabbi?" (2)

THE CLAIMS OF JESUS IN LUKE'S GOSPEL

• Jesus showed his power over nature.
"The disciples went and woke him [Jesus], saying, 'Master, Master, we're going to drown!' He got up and rebuked the wind and the raging waters; the storm subsided, and all was calm." *Luke 8:24*

THE CLAIMS OF JESUS IN JOHN'S GOSPEL

• Jesus claimed to be the world's Light.
"I am the light of the world. Whoever follows me will never walk in darkness, but will have the light of life." *John 8:12*

• Jesus claimed to be able to give people eternal life.
"Whoever drinks the water I give him will never thirst. Indeed, the water I give him will become in him a spring of water welling up to eternal life. *John 4:14*

• Jesus claimed to exist before Abraham's time.
"'I tell you the truth,' Jesus answered, 'before Abraham was born, I am!'" *John 8:58*

• Jesus claimed to be one with the Father.
"I and the Father are one." *John 10:30*

• Jesus accepted the worship of people.
"Thomas said to him [Jesus], 'My Lord and my God.'" *John 20:28*

JESUS' CLAIMS TO BE GOD

The clearest of Jesus' spoken claims to deity found anywhere in the New Testament come in John's Gospel, chapter five.

He was God in the form of a human being:	*John 5:17-18*
He had power to raise the dead:	*John 5:21, 28-29*
He would be the future judge of all people:	*John 5:22*
He claimed equal honor with God:	*John 5:23*
He was able to give life to people, in place of death:	*John 5:24*

WHAT'S THE CONCLUSION?

The question which Jesus asked his disciples, "Who do you say I am?" (*Matthew 16:15*), is the query we have to answer. The best place to find the answer is within the pages of the four Gospels.

We're not responsible for what leading theologians believe. In many ways they have divergent views about Jesus, just as the leading theologians had in Jesus' own day. We are responsible, though, to come to a firm conclusion of whether we believe or disbelieve the claims about Jesus.

"How can a person today come to really know who Jesus is?"

WHAT'S THE PROBLEM?
"Christians claim to 'know' Jesus in some way. How can a person who knows next to nothing about Christianity find out about Jesus? And anyway, how can you 'know' someone who's dead?"

LOOK AT THE NAMES OF JESUS

You can discover the personality and characteristics of Jesus by noting the different names given to him in the New Testament.

Name	Quotation
1. The Almighty	"I am … the Almighty."
2. Great God	"The glorious appearing of our great God."
3. Savior	"The glorious appearing of our … Savior."
4. Word	"In the beginning was the Word."
5. Alpha andOmega	"I am the Alpha and the Omega."
6. The Christ (anointed)	"You are the Christ."
7. Jesus (personal name on earth)	"You are to give him the name Jesus."
8. The Son of God	"In the knowledge of the Son of God."
9. Immanuel	"They will call him Immanuel."
10. The Way	"I am the way."
11. The Truth	"I am the truth."
12. The Life	"I am the life."
13. Lord of lords	"He is Lord of lords."
14. King of kings	"He is … King of kings."
15. Shepherd	"You have returned to the Shepherd."
16. Lamb of God	"Look, the Lamb of God."

DECIPHER EACH NAME

As you read through the names, ask yourself, "What does this particular name tell me about Jesus?"

KNOWING JESUS IS MORE THAN KNOWING ABOUT JESUS

Christians believe that Jesus is alive now. He cannot yet be known face-to-face but he has promised that his Spirit, given to each Christian, reveals who he is in a person-to-person encounter.

> "If you love me, you will obey what I command. And I will ask the Father, and he will give you another Counselor to be with you for ever – the Spirit of truth. The world cannot accept him, because it neither sees him nor knows him. But you know him, for he lives with you and will be in you. I will not leave you as orphans; I will come to you."
> *John 14:15-18*

WHAT'S THE CONCLUSION?

Read the Gospels asking for the help of the Spirit to discover and to know the reality of the living Jesus. Don't be satisfied in just knowing about Jesus. Get to know him in a personal way.

A QUOTE TO CHEW OVER

> "Read the Gospels, and allow God to whisper in your minds and into your hearts words that can have a profound effect on the way we think and act. He will find us if we listen to his voice calling to us through the fog that often surrounds us, a kind of cloud of unknowing, and above the noise that muffles his call."
> *Cardinal Basil Hume*

Bible reference

Revelation 1:8
Titus 2:13
Titus 2:13
John 1:1
Revelation 1:8
Matthew 16:16
Matthew 1:21
Ephesians 4:13
Matthew 1:23
John 14:6
John 14:6
John 14:6
Revelation 17:14
Revelation 17:14
1 Peter 2:25
John 1:29

"Won't Christianity cramp my style?"

WHAT'S THE PROBLEM?
"I'm into being free. I'm sure that Christianity would restrict or hinder me too much. Won't I lose my freedom if I become a Christian?"

THE TRUTH OF CHRISTIANITY BRINGS FREEDOM NOT BONDAGE

Christianity has been responsible for setting people free:

• **Freedom from disease.** Pioneer medical missionaries started the first hospitals in many countries.

• **Freedom from injustice.** Martin Luther King Jr was a fervent and devout Baptist preacher who never lost his Christian convictions as he battled for racial equality in America.

• **Freedom from neglect and homelessness.** The founder of the Salvation Army, William Booth, started to care for the physical and spiritual welfare of the poor in London's down-town East End while he was an evangelist.

QUESTION: "What about my personal freedom? Will I lose that?"

The answer to this question is both "yes" and "no".

"Yes"
If you go Christ's way in preference to your own path you will lose some things:

• You may lose some friends.
• You may be jeered by some who now look down upon you.
• You may need to change your ambition and priorities in life.
• You may wish to stop doing some things you were doing before.

"No"
• In reality, what you thought was personal freedom was in actuality a personal bondage.
• "You may think you are the captain of your soul, but, in fact, you are your ship's worst passenger." *Aldous Huxley*

QUESTION: "In what ways can Jesus make me free?"

God created you. God knows all about you. He knows what is best for you.

You might compare the freedom in Christ to the freedom on a weight-loss diet. Before the diet, you were a slave to food and its gratification. This resulted in extra weight, possible physical problems and unhappiness. But with the diet came restrictions, but also tremendous freedoms. The freedom to choose new clothes; the freedom to feel good physically; and the freedom to feel good about yourself. Dieting discipline, at first, seems restrictive but the end is freedom and happiness. In the same way, Christ brings new freedoms and joys never before experienced.

Jesus once said, "I seek not to please myself but him [God] who sent me" (*John 5:30*). If you followed that way of living would you find yourself being freed from certain strangleholds of:
- covetousness?
- wishing the downfall of others?
- seeking revenge?
- nursing grudges?
- addiction?
- greed?
- fear?

Regulations versus relationships

Christianity is not a set of rules. "Thou shalt not do this, thou shalt not do that." Christianity's focus is on knowing a person – Jesus Christ – and enjoying a friendship with him.

QUESTION: "How does this work out in practice?"

Through Christ a new power source is available – the Holy Spirit, and a new motivation is put within us. This was Paul's experience. *See Romans 7:25; 8:2.*

WHAT'S THE CONCLUSION?

"'Be yourself,' is about the worst advice you can give to people."
Mark Twain

A QUOTE TO CHEW OVER

Jesus said:
"I tell you the truth, everyone who sins is a slave to sin. Now a slave has no permanent place in the family, but a son belongs to it for ever. So if the Son sets you free, you will be free indeed."
John 8:34-36

"Isn't it true that only weaklings need Christianity?"

WHAT'S THE PROBLEM?
"Isn't Christianity just a crutch for the inadequate and feeble? If so, I don't want to have anything to do with it."

JUST HOW STRONG ARE WE?
Flip on the evening news and what do you see reported? Man's inhumanity to man. So called "ethnic cleansing" (nothing less than mass murder). Kids abused, girls raped. Greed. Dog eat dog. Thinly disguised lust for power.

JUST HOW STRONG AM I AS AN INDIVIDUAL?
Have you never wished to be rid of you own personal shortcomings – cutting words – a self-centered lifestyle – shameful actions?

THE BIBLE'S ANALYSIS OF HUMAN NATURE
It is warped:

> "The heart is deceitful above all things." *Jeremiah 17:9*

CHRISTIANITY HAS BEEN CALLED A "RESCUE" RELIGION
When criticized for sharing a meal with tax collectors and sinners, Jesus told the Pharisees: "It is not the healthy who need a doctor, but the sick." *Matthew 9:12*

Jesus came to give spiritual healing as well as physical healing.

WHO JESUS CANNOT HELP

There is only one group of people Jesus is unable to help – the self-satisfied, the complacent. If you can't admit that you are spiritually sick, you probably won't seek healing. Jesus said that he had come, "to heal the sick" *Luke 9:2* But if you feel totally inadequate you're definitely in need of a divine Healer. It takes enormous inner honesty to admit that you need help. It takes humility to seek out Jesus and admit that you're a "weak" person.

WHAT'S THE CONCLUSION?

"The only wisdom we can hope to acquire is the wisdom of humility." *T.S. Eliot*

A QUOTE TO CHEW OVER

One of the mottoes of Paul, the first century pioneer missionary, was:

"I can do everything through him [Christ] who gives me strength." *Philippians 4:13*

"Isn't the church full of hypocrites?"

WHAT'S THE PROBLEM?
"Why should I become a Christian and go to church? Aren't the worst hypocrites in the world packing out the churches?"

Look at the history of Christianity
Christianity through the centuries is littered with examples of downright evil! It's more than just hypocrites today.

- The Crusades – during which thousands of innocent people were killed in the name of Christ.

- The Spanish Inquisition – when people had their bodies tortured, purportedly, to save their souls from hell.

- Catholics have burnt Protestants at the stake.
- Protestants have burnt Catholics at the stake.

Examples of hypocrisy today

- The tele-evangelists whose primary motivation seems to be money.

- The married minister who runs off with the choir director.

- The business man who teaches a Bible class, but swindles money at work.

WHAT IS THE DIFFERENCE BETWEEN A CHRISTIAN, A SINNER AND A HYPOCRITE?

A Christian is a sinner who has been forgiven and cleansed of sin. Christ's death and resurrection provides forgiveness – past, present and future. Even though he or she has received forgiveness, he or she continues to fall into sin. The battle against sin continues, even as a Christian.

> "If we claim to be without sin, we deceive ourselves and the truth is not in us. If we confess our suns, he is faithful and just and will forgive us our sins and purify us from all unrighteousness." 1 JOHN 1:8-9

A sinner is a person who has never experienced any forgiveness or removal of sin by God. Forgiveness is readily available (just like a gift), but the sinner has never claimed God's gift of absolution and pardon.

A hypocrite may well be a Christian but his or her Christian testimony conflicts with the way he or she lives – there is a certain falseness about his or her profession of faith. It is this falseness that Jesus condemned when he spoke to the religious leaders.

> "And when you pray, do not be like the hypocrites, for they love to pray standing in the synagogues and on the street corners to be seen by men." MATTHEW 6:5

CHRISTIANITY DOES NOT STAND OR FALL BY THE BEHAVIOR OF CHRISTIANS

It is tragic when scandals are unearthed among Christians. What a terrible advertisement for Christianity.

However, the truth of Christianity is not shattered by such hypocrisy. **The truth of Christianity stands or falls by the person of the Lord Jesus Christ.**

THE HYPOCRITES OF JESUS' DAY

In Jesus' day hypocrisy was rampant – hypocrites infested the leadership of the religious groups.

> "Woe to you, teachers of the law and Pharisees, you hypocrites! You shut the kingdom of heaven in men's faces. You yourselves do not enter, nor will you let those enter who are trying to."
> *Matthew 23:13*

JESUS HAD NO TIME FOR HYPOCRITES

Outwardly, these religious leaders were very pious but inwardly they were not pious at all – they were wicked.

> "On the outside you appear to people as righteous but on the inside you are full of hypocrisy and wickedness."
> *Matthew 23:28*

Jesus reserved his harshest words for these religious hypocrites.

> "You snakes! You brood of vipers! How will you escape being condemned to hell?"
> *Matthew 23:33*

ADVICE to the person who is genuinely worried about hypocrisy in the church

Someone has said, "When you find the perfect church, don't join it, as it will then no longer be perfect."

WHAT'S THE CONCLUSION?

There shouldn't be hypocrisy in the church, but there is. Even so, its presence does not invalidate Christianity.

A QUOTE TO CHEW OVER

The Indian Christian, Sundar Singh, once asked Mahatma Ghandi how Christianity could capture India. Ghandi replied:

> "You Christians must begin to live like Jesus Christ. You must practice your religion without adulterating it or toning it down. You must put your emphasis on love: for love is the center and soul of Christianity."

> "I have seen Christianity and it doesn't work." *Mahatma Ghandi*

"If Christianity is so wonderful, why are there so few Christians?"

WHAT'S THE PROBLEM?
"If everything that Christians claim for Christianity were true, wouldn't the whole world become Christian?"

IT'S NOT ALL BAD NEWS
There are revivals around the world.

- About a third of the people in the world claim some kind of allegiance to Christianity.
- The areas of the world which enjoy a great increase in the number of Christians are often forgotten about:
- In China millions are turning to Christ.
- In Africa a number of countries are experiencing exciting revivals.
- In South America the Christian churches are expanding much faster than in Europe or Northern America.

FEW OF THE CHRISTIANS HAD ANY SOCIAL STANDING
"Brothers, think of what you were when you were called.
Not many of you were wise by human standards;
not many were influential; not many were of noble birth.
But God chose foolish things of the world to shame the wise;
God chose the weak things of the world to shame the strong."
1 Corinthians 1:26-27

SO WHY ISN'T EVERYONE A CHRISTIAN?
- Some people reject Christ because they have intellectual problems with Christianity.
- Some people reject Christ because, while they know all about Christianity, they are not prepared to admit that they are sinners before God.
- Some people reject Christianity because it's so humbling. Simple childlike, (not childish), faith in Jesus is not for them. "He [Jesus] called a little child and had him stand among them. And he said, 'I tell you the truth, unless you change and become like little children, you will never enter the kingdom of heaven.'" *Matthew 18:2-3*
- Some people reject Christianity because they have no sense of need.
- Some people reject Christianity because they can't be bothered to think it through.

THERE ARE SOME REALLY EVIL PEOPLE AROUND

Christians have always been persecuted. Every century has seen hundreds of thousands of Christians martyred at the hands of godless and wicked men. Such evil people, wrote Paul, "suppress the truth by their wickedness." *Romans 1:18*

WHAT'S THE CONCLUSION?

Christians remain in the minority today, and this fact has always been true. But, unlike some of us, Jesus never seemed to have been worried about the small number of people who followed him.

> "Enter through the narrow gate. For wide is the gate and broad is the road that leads to destruction, and many enter through it. But small is the gate and narrow the road that leads to life, and only a few find it." *Matthew 7:13-14*

A QUOTE TO CHEW OVER

> "The heart of the problem is the problem of the heart." *Anonymous*

"You can't even prove the existence of God, can you?" (1)

WHAT'S THE PROBLEM?
"Prove to me that God exists – and I'll believe. But you can't, can you?"

CAN ANYONE PROVE THAT GOD EXISTS?
The straightforward answer is: No. The Bible never sets out to prove his existence. The Bible always assumes his existence.

The Bible starts off with the statement, "In the beginning God…" *Genesis 1:1*

ANSELM TRIED

Anselm, 1033-1109, a leading Christian philosopher and theologian was the first person to come up with the **ontological** argument for the existence of God. The word *ontological* comes from the Greek word meaning 'being'. Anselm believed that God was the "greatest conceivable being."

Anselm tried to prove the existence of God by reason. He defined God as "something greater than anything else that could be conceived."

AQUINAS TRIED

Thomas Aquinas, 1225–74, used the **cosmological** argument to prove the existence of God. The Greek word *kosmos* means universe, world or order. The cosmological argument states that everything that exists had a First Cause, and that this First Cause is God.

Aquinas also used the **teleological** argument. The Greek word *telos* means purpose or goal. The teleological argument focuses on the argument from design. As a watch suggests a watchmaker, so the evidence of design in our world points to the Creator God.

A QUOTE TO CHEW OVER

Anselm taught that faith must move us towards using our minds in the right way.

> "I am not seeking to understand in order to believe, but I believe in order that I may understand. For this too I believe: that unless I believe, I shall not understand." *Anselm*

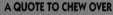

"You can't even prove the existence of God, can you?" (2)

THOMAS AQUINAS TRIED TO "PROVE" THE EXISTENCE OF GOD
Aquinas, 1225-1274, was the greatest theologian of his day.

AQUINAS' FIVE WAYS

1. The Argument From Motion
1. Nothing can move itself.
2. If every object in motion had a mover, then the first object in motion needed a mover.
3. This first mover is the Unmoved Mover, called God.

2. Causation Of Existence
1. There exist things that are caused (created) by other things.
2. Nothing can be the cause of itself (nothing can create itself.)
3. There can not be an endless string of objects causing other objects to exist.
4. Therefore, there must be an uncaused first cause called God.

3. Contingent and Necessary Objects
This Principle or Way defines two types of objects in the universe: contingent beings and necessary beings. A contingent being is an object that cannot exist without a necessary being causing its existence. Aquinas believed that the existence of contingent beings would ultimately necessitate a being which must exist for all of the contingent beings to exist. This being, called a necessary being, is God.
1. Contingent beings are caused.
2. Not every being can be contingent.

3. There must exist a being which is necessary to cause contingent beings.
4. This necessary being is God.

4. The Argument From Degrees And Perfection
Thomas formulated this Principle from a very interesting observation about the qualities of things. For example, one may say that of two marble sculptures one is more beautiful than the other, one has a greater degree of beauty than the next. This is referred to as degrees or gradation of a quality. From this fact Aquinas concluded that for any given quality (e.g. goodness, beauty, knowledge) there must be a perfect standard by which all such qualities are measured. These perfections are contained in God.

5. The Argument From Intelligent Design
The final Principle that St. Thomas Aquinas speaks of has to do with the observable universe and the order of nature. Aquinas states that common sense tells us that the universe works in such a way, that one can conclude that it was designed by an intelligent designer, God. In other words, all physical laws and the order of nature and life were designed and ordered by God, the intelligent designer.

BY WAY OF ILLUSTRATION

A man found a watch in a bush. He picked it up as he had never seen one before. He saw how the hands moved in a logical way. He opened the back and found cogs, springs, jewels, levers and wheels. He then discovered how to make it work as he wound it up. He saw that the complex machinery moved to a predetermined pattern.

He thought to himself: "I've found this watch. There must be a watchmaker somewhere."

This man then thought about the world, with is regular four successive seasons, and the silent planets zooming around on their paths.

He thought to himself: "The world must have a maker as well."

TWO BOOKS

Psalm 19 says:
1. Look at the book of nature. *Psalm 19:1-6*
2. Look at the book of the law (for us the Bible).
   Psalm 19:7-11

A QUOTE TO CHEW OVER

"The truth of the Christian faith … surpasses the capacity of reason, nevertheless that truth that the human reason is naturally endowed to know can not be opposed to the truth of the Christian faith." *Aquinas*

"Can I be a Christian without losing my intellectual integrity?"

WHAT'S THE PROBLEM?
"Isn't Christianity just for those who indulge in wishful thinking? Can anyone with a good brain embrace Christianity without leaving his critical faculties behind?"

"ASSASSINATING" YOUR BRAIN
Christians are sometimes said to have "assassinated their brains". This is especially so if they say they believe in things like miracles, the resurrection of Jesus and the divine inspiration of the Bible.

USE YOUR MIND

Intelligence should never be a barrier to belief in God. Intelligence should be an asset to belief.

> "And when Jesus saw that he had answered intelligently, He said to him, 'You are not far from the kingdom of God.'"
> *Mark 12:34, NASB*

INTELLECTUAL INTEGRITY AND THE OLD TESTAMENT
The Israelites were told to intellectually ignore any prophet who gave false predictions.

> "If what a prophet proclaims in the name of the Lord does not take place or come true, that is a message the Lord has not spoken. That prophet has spoken presumptuously. Do not be afraid of him." *Deuteronomy 18:22*

DOES FAITH HAVE TO BE UNINTELLIGENT?
Absolutely not. In fact Christians are encouraged to intellectually test all things. They are told to keep their wits about them and to assess everything that appears to be coming from God to determine whether the messages are true or false. Christians are required to intellectually investigate everything they are told.

- Paul said: "Test everything." *1 Thessalonians 5:21*

- John said: "Do not believe every spirit, but test the spirits to see whether they are from God, because many false prophets have gone out into the world." *1 John 4:1*
- Jesus said: "At that time if anyone says to you, 'Look, here is the Christ!' or, 'There he is!' do not believe it. For false Christs and false prophets will appear and perform great signs and miracles to deceive even the elect – if that were possible.'" *Matthew 24:23-24*

WE ARE TO LOVE GOD WITH OUR MINDS

The Old Testament command says:	Jesus said:
"Love the Lord your God	Love the Lord your God
with all your heart	with all your heart
and with all your souland	with all your soul
and with all your strength."	and with all your *mind*."
Deuteronomy 6:5	*Matthew 22:37*

A QUOTE TO CHEW OVER

"God has room for people with very little sense. But he wants everyone to use whatever sense they have. The proper motto is not, 'Be good, sweet maid, and let who can be clever,' but, 'Be good, sweet maid, and don't forget that this involves being as clever as you can.' God is no fonder of intellectual slackers than of any other slackers." *C.S. Lewis*

"Isn't it against our rational makeup to have blind faith as Christians do?"

WHAT'S THE PROBLEM?
"Oil and water don't mix. Faith and reason don't mix. Doesn't it go against reason to make a leap of faith into the dark?"

IS CHRISTIAN BELIEF BASED ON IGNORANCE?
• Christian faith is based on observable facts

> "Jesus did many other miraculous signs in the presence of his disciples, which are not recorded in this book. But these are written that you may believe that Jesus is the Christ, the Son of God, and that by believing you may have life in his name."
> *John 20:30-31*

• There is firm evidence for Jesus' resurrection

> "After his suffering, he [Jesus] showed himself to these men [his apostles] and gave many convincing proofs that he was alive. He appeared to them over a period of forty days and spoke about the kingdom of God." *Acts 1:3*

YOUR MIND MATTERS
• Christians are encouraged to keep on growing in their knowledge and understanding

> "And this is my prayer: that your love may abound more and more in knowledge and depth of insight, so that you may be able to discern what is best and may be pure and blameless until the day of Christ." *Philippians 1:9-10*

• Christians are sensible people and are to make judgments.

> "I speak to sensible people; judge for yourselves what I say."
> *1 Corinthians 10:15*

FAITH IS...

> "Now faith is being sure of what we hope for and certain of what we do not see."
> *Hebrews 11:1*

CHECK IT OUT
The first Christians did not approach skeptics with the message, "Just believe." They told them to investigate the factual and historical foundation of the Christian faith. The Bereans were commended for doing just this:

> "Now the Bereans were of more noble character than the Thessalonians, for they

received the message with great eagerness and examined the Scriptures every day to see if what Paul said was true."
Acts 17:11

Christianity says that faith is placing one's confidence in Jesus. This faith is based on historical, knowable facts, not on false hopes.

FAITH

Becoming a Christian is more than an intellectual decision. God is far greater than the human mind. The very concept of Christianity is awe-inspiring and mysterious. There are heights and depths that are beyond the ability of the mind to fathom. This all demands faith – which is a confident belief in the trruth of a person or idea, even when it may not seem logical.

FROM UNBELIEF TO FAITH

Many people who initially rejected the Christian faith came to embrace Christianity by carefully studying the facts which Christianity claims to be founded on.

It was not through blind faith.

Two good examples of skeptics who became believers are lawyer Frank Morrison, author of *Who Moved the Stone?*, and Lew Wallace, the author of *Ben Hur*.

WHAT'S THE CONCLUSION?
Don't approach Christianity like a dumb, senseless brute beast

"I will instruct you and teach you in the way you should go.
I will counsel you and watch over you.
Do not be like the horse or the mule,
which have no understanding
but must be controlled with bit and bridle
or they will not come to you."
Psalm 32:8-9

A QUOTE TO CHEW OVER

"Happy are those who go forward not by sight but by the trust of faith." *Brother Roger of Taizé*

"Why bother to pray?"

WHAT'S THE PROBLEM?
"Does God really listen to us when we pray? If he doesn't, then what's the point in praying? If he does hear us, he already knew what we were going to pray about, so, again, why pray? Can you tell me why there are so many unanswered prayers."

WHAT ABOUT SO-CALLED UNANSWERED PRAYERS?
God always answers prayers but his answer isn't always "Yes". Sometimes his answer may be "No", or "Wait".

God even said "No" to Paul. He prayed not once but three times for God to remove an ailment, his "thorn in the flesh". But it was not taken away.

> "To keep me from being conceited because of these surprisingly great revelations, there was given me a thorn in my flesh, a messenger of Satan, to torment me. Three times I pleaded with the Lord to take it away from me. But he said to me, 'My grace is sufficient for you, for my power is made perfect in weakness.'" *2 Corinthians 12:7-9*

QUESTIONS ABOUT PRAYER
1. What words should I use?
2. What do I do when I feel like giving up on prayer altogether?
3. How can the Holy Spirit help me with my prayers?

Just because we may never fathom how prayer "works" that is no good reason to stop praying.

THERE IS MUCH MORE TO PRAYER THAN ASKING FOR THINGS
Prayer is about connecting to God and learning to love him. It is about being God-centered and about learning to look at life from God's perspective. It is about finding out what God wants.

JESUS ENCOURAGED HIS FOLLOWERS TO PRAY TO GOD
Jesus instructed his disciples how they should pray. He gave them the words of what's called the Lord's Prayer (*Matthew 6:9-13*). Jesus told his disciples to persevere in prayer.

> "Then Jesus told his disciples a parable to show them that they should always pray and not give up." *Luke 18:1*

HELP FROM THE HOLY SPIRIT

"In the same way, the Spirit helps us in our weakness.
We do not know what we ought to pray for,
but the Spirit himself intercedes for us
with groans that words cannot express."
Romans 8:26

"The best prayers have more often groans that words."
John Bunyan

A QUOTE TO CHEW OVER

"My secret is quite
simple.
I pray."
*Mother
Teresa*

"What's the difference between a cult and a mainstream Church?"

WHAT'S THE PROBLEM?
"How can I identify a dangerous religious group?"

1. Beware of groups which reject the authority of Scripture

Also beware of groups who distort the teaching of Scripture by unduly emphasizing or misreading certain passages.

The biblical teaching of the apostles and other divinely inspired authors of Scripture must never be rejected.

"What you heard from me, keep as the pattern of sound teaching, with faith and love in Christ Jesus. Guard the good deposit that was entrusted to you – guard it with the help of the Holy Spirit who lives in us."
2 Timothy 1:13-14

A QUESTION TO ASK
Does the group consider any other documents of equal or greater importance than Scripture?

TELL-TALE SIGNS
Cults often deny one or more basic Christian doctrines, such as:
• The Trinity
• The deity of Christ
• Salvation by grace alone through faith in Jesus
• The bodily resurrection of Jesus

2. Beware of groups which have unbiblical leadership Jesus gave this warning about false prophets:

"Watch out for false prophets. They come to you in sheep's clothing, but inwardly they are ferocious wolves. By their fruit you will recognize them. Do people pick grapes from thornbushes, or figs from thistles? Likewise every good tree bears good fruit, but a bad tree bears bad fruit. A good tree cannot bear bad fruit, and a bad tree cannot bear good fruit.

Every tree that does not bear good fruit is cut down and thrown into the fire. Thus, by their fruit you will recognize them." *Matthew 7:15-20*

QUALITIES TO LOOK FOR IN GOOD CHRISTIAN LEADERS

They are not given over to obvious vices.

"The overseer must be …
• the husband of one wife,
• temperate,
• self-controlled,
• respectable,
• hospitable,
• able to teach not given over to drunkenness,
• not violent but gentle,
• not quarrelsome,
• not a lover of money,
• he must manage his own family well."

1 Timothy 3:2-4

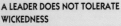

A LEADER DOES NOT TOLERATE WICKEDNESS

"Have nothing to do with the fruitless deeds of darkness, but rather expose them."
Ephesians 5:11

A LEADER IS STILL A SERVANT

Jesus said, "I, your Lord and Teacher, have washed your feet, you should also wash one anothers' feet."
John 13:14

TELL-TALE SIGN

• Cult leaders often claim excessive personal authority.

3. Beware of groups which separate themselves from outsiders

It is true that Christians are told: "Do not be yoked together with unbelievers." And, "come out from them and be separate." (*2 Corinthians 6:14,17*). But Christian groups should not isolate themselves from the world in unbiblical ways.

TELL-TALE SIGNS

• Groups which encourage members to avoid contact with other Christians.
• Groups which encourage members to cut off from their families.

A QUOTE TO CHEW OVER

"I tell you the truth, the man who does not enter the sheep pen by the gate, but climbs in by some other way, is a thief and a robber." *John 10:1*

"Should Christians give away all their possessions?"

WHAT'S THE PROBLEM?
"Jesus told one rich young man who came to him to give all his possessions to the poor and follow him. Does this mean that everyone who follows Jesus needs to give everything away? Isn't that what Francis of Assisi did?"

JESUS AND THE RICH YOUNG MAN
Jesus was clear about what this young man should do.

> "Jesus looked at him and loved him. 'One thing you lack,' he said. 'Go, sell everything you have and give to the poor, and you will have treasure in heaven. Then come, follow me."
> *Mark 10:21*

Points to note
1. Jesus didn't tell everyone to sell everything.
2. The young man's unwillingness to sell his possessions revealed that he was not prepared to follow Jesus.

RICHES
There are plenty of warnings in the Bible about being gripped by the love of money.

PAUL	THE PSALMIST	JESUS
"For the love of money is a root of all kinds of evil. Some people, eager for money, have wandered from the faith and pierced themselves with many griefs" *1 Timothy 6:10*	"Though your riches increase, do not set your heart on them." *Psalm 62:10*	"It is easier for a camel to go through the eye of a needle than for a rich man to enter the kingdom of God." *Mark 10:25*

THE EARLY CHURCH

Didn't the first Christians practice "Christian communism"?

"All the believers were together and had everything in common. Selling their possessions and goods, they gave to anyone as he had need."
Acts 2:44-45

Points to note:

1. There was no compulsion for everyone to sell everything.
2. Not all Christians sold their houses. See Acts 12:12

How they gave money

"Each man should give what he has decided in his heart to give. And God is able to make all grace about to you, so that in all things at all times, having all that you need, you well abound in every good work."
2 Corinthians 9:7-8

WHAT'S THE CONCLUSION?

Nowhere does the Bible teach that we should neglect our own families.

"If anyone does not provide for his relatives, and especially for his immediate family, he has denied the faith and is worse than an unbeliever." *1 Timothy 5:8*

A QUOTE TO CHEW OVER

"I don't believe one can settle how much we ought to give. I'm afraid the only safe rule is to give more than we can spare."
C.S. Lewis

"What makes you say that Jesus is the only way to God?"

WHAT'S THE PROBLEM?
- "Are Christians so rude as to ignore other faiths?
- "Are Christians so ignorant as to say that there is no good in other faiths?
- "Are Christians so superior that they have to say that Jesus is the only way to God?"

PETER'S BLOCKBUSTER STATEMENT
Peter and John were hauled up before the Sanhedrin. They grilled Peter and John: "By what power or what name did you do this [heal a cripple]?" (*Acts 4:7*). Peter replied when he was "filled with the Holy Spirit" (*Acts 4:8*). He did not say, "Any good religion is OK," but said:

> "Salvation is found in no one else, [than in Jesus Christ of Nazareth] for there is no other name under heaven given to men by which we must be saved." *Acts 4:12*

PAUL'S STATEMENT

> "For there is one God and one mediator between God and men, the man Christ Jesus." *1 Timothy 2:5*

THE WARNING GIVEN BY THE WRITER TO THE HEBREWS

"How shall we escape if we ignore such a great salvation?"
Hebrews 2:3

WHAT'S THE CONCLUSION?

Towards the end of each Gospel there is a command for
Christians to go out and spread the Christian message.

Matthew	"Go and make disciples of all nations."	*Matthew 28:19*
Mark	"Go into all the world and preach the good news [about Jesus] to all creation."	*Mark 16:15*
Luke	"Repentance and forgiveness of sins will be preached in his [Jesus'] name to all nations, beginning at Jerusalem. You are witnesses of these things."	*Luke 24:47-48*
John	"You also must testify about me."	*John 15:27*

A QUOTE TO CHEW OVER

"I take it that a religion which claims to be following the
truth, the whole truth and nothing but the truth must, even if
only by a process of elimination, think that the other religions
are, for all their holiness and worship, mistaken. ... It is
surely reasonable to ask Christianity what its founder meant
when he said, "None shall come to the Father but by me." I
do not offer these words to give offence, but many a devout
Christian is worried by them, and many a bishop, opening
his heart to other faiths, must be hard put to it to provide an
answer."
Bernard Levin in The Times (27.1.92)

"How can the death of one man 2,000 years ago help me today?"

WHAT'S THE PROBLEM?

"I can accept the fact that Jesus' death was an historical event. But that happened 2,000 years ago. How can an event like that be of any use to me in the 21st century?"

WHO DIED?

This wasn't just another criminal. This man on the Roman cross, going through such an excruciatingly painful death, was not just another criminal.

It was the eternal Son of God who was crucified.

PAST, PRESENT, FUTURE

On that Good Friday the death of Jesus, often predicted by himself, was like no other death, before or since.

It affected all time – past, present and future.

WHY DID JESUS DIE?

Jesus never said that the main purpose of his death was to show us how to be a perfect martyr. When he died on the cross he died so that our sins could be forgiven. Paul explained to the Christians at Ephesus what was happening during the crucifixion in these words:

"In him [Jesus] we have redemption through his blood [death], the forgiveness of sins." *Ephesians 1:7*

OUR SINS ARE "COVERED"

The Psalmist is fond of explaining that our sins are forgiven by saying that our sins are "covered" by God.

"You forgave the iniquity of your people and covered all their sins." *Psalm 85:2*

"Blessed is he whose transgressions are forgiven, whose sins are covered." *Psalm 32:1*

WHAT ABOUT THOSE WHO LIVED BEFORE JESUS?

Since the death of Jesus is an eternal fact, the benefits to be derived from his death affect those who lived before him as well as those who lived after him.

BY WAY OF ILLUSTRATION

"There is a village in the middle of England called Shireoaks, so named because of a famous tree ('The Shire Oak') which marked the point at which three counties met – Yorkshire, Nottinghamshire and Derbyshire. It was a remarkable tree and of great historic interest, until it was cut down at the end of the eighteenth century. Its diameter was about thirty yards, and it was said to be able to shelter over 200 horses. Its branches spread into all three counties, and in each of them you could stand beneath its shade.

"It is like that with the cross, the death of Jesus. It is an eternal fact embracing the whole of history, and those who lived in the past, or were alive at the time, or who have been born since, may through faith enjoy its benefits."
John Eddison, Who Died Why? Scripture Union

A quote to chew over

"Jesus became the greatest liar, perjurer, thief, adulterer and murderer that mankind has ever known – not because he committed these sins but because he was actually made sin for us." *Martin Luther*

"Can Christianity help me, I'm a doubter?"

WHAT'S THE PROBLEM?
"Other people seem to have such a strong faith. My faith always seems to be so weak and feeble. How can Christianity help someone with shallow faith?"

WHAT DO YOU DOUBT?
Try to determine the sources of your problems and doubts. Write them down in a notebook. Then seek answers to your doubts from studying the Bible, through prayer, from reading Christian books, and from talking with other Christians.

A DIFFICULTY MAY NOT BE A DOUBT AND ALL DOUBTS ARE NOT WRONG

"Ten thousand difficulties do not make one doubt."
J.H. Newman

"One must know when it is right to doubt, to affirm, to submit. Anyone who does otherwise does not understand the force of reason." *Blaise Pascal*

"It is not as a child that I believe and confess Christ. My hosanna is born of a furnace of doubt." *Fyodor Dostoevsky*

Jesus was gentle with doubting Thomas and gave him the help he needed. See John 20:24-29.

WHAT'S THE CONCLUSION?

"There lives more faith in honest doubt believe me, than in half the creeds."
Tennyson In Memoriam

A QUOTE TO CHEW OVER

"It's not great faith that is required, but faith in a great God." *Anonymous*